FIGHTING
TO BREATHE

Jong Yi

FIGHTING TO BREATHE

Recommend to read with parents for kids age 13 and older.

Paperback (ISBN): 978-163944993-4
Ebook (ISBN): 978-0-578-24668-0
Library of Congress Control Number: 2021906058

Copy Editor: *Taryn Wieland*
Cover and interior design: *Marites D. Bautista*
Cover photo purchased by: *Jong Yi*

CONTENTS